LEEK &
MANIFOLD V
LIGHT RAILWAY

Lindsey Porter

INTRODUCTION

Most days of the year, even when the weather is bad, visitors can be found walking and cycling along the Manifold and Hamps Valleys between Waterhouses in the south and Hulme End in the north. It is a distance of eight miles and the path they use is covered with tarmac.

It is the track bed of the Leek & Manifold Valley Light Railway, which ran between 1904 and 1934. Several books have been written about the history of the line. Yet for those who are not ardent railway enthusiasts, there is currently no title in print which satisfies the casual visitor's curiosity. This book's object is to satisfy that need. With the use of period photographs, chiefly of the railway but also of nearby villages, the days of the L&MVLR are brought back for us.

The popularity today of this little line stems perhaps because of the nostalgia for things gone by and its superb location. It must also be because of the unusual nature of the railway. It was narrow guage, built to a rail width of thirty inches. The engines were of a very similar design to those on the Barsi Light Railway in India. Even the coaches were colonial in style. They were painted primrose yellow and must have been quite picturesque when seen down the valley.

This collection of phototgraphs will, I hope, give a good pictorial record of what there was and what could have been today, had the line survived the years of the Depression and the war that followed it. I hope you enjoy them.

Lindsey Porter

© CLM Porter 2002

ACKNOWLEDGEMENTS

I wish to thank Derbyshire Life & Countryside of Derby for use of their photograph of the train at Beeston Tor and Basil Jeuda for the Nithsdale postcard of three valley scenes. The cover was painted by Tony Beresford of Underhill Farm, Buxton Road, Longnor, Nr Buxton, Derbyshire SK17 0PU. Designed by Mark Titterton.

British Library Cataloguing in Publication Data: A catalogue record for this book is available from the British Library.

Printed in England by Bookcraft, Midsomer Norton, Somerset

The number of documents associated with the establishment of the railway was perhaps more than may be realised. Here are a selection. Some relate to operating, borrowing, as well as the shares prospectus (see p.4).

1898.

✸

The Leek & Manifold Valley Light Railway Company.

(Incorporated by Order of the Light Railway Commissioners under the Light Railways Act 1896).

Supported by a Free Grant of £10,000 from Her Majesty's Treasury and a Loan of £10,000 from the Staffordshire County Council.

Share Capital = = £15,000

(with power to increase to £20,000).

Issue of 15,000 *Ordinary Shares of* £1 *each payable as follows:*

2/6 per Share on application.
2/6 do. on allotment.
5/- do. 3 months after allotment.

And the balance in calls of not more than 5/- per share, at intervals of at least 3 months, as the construction of the Railway proceeds.

Directors.

CHAS. BILL, Esq., M.P., J.P., C.A., Woodhouse, Cheadle, Staffs., and 16 Hans Mansions, S.W.

JOHN BREALEY, Esq., J.P., Leek, Staffs.

FRANK DREWRY, Esq., J.P., Buxton, Derbyshire.

ALFRED HALL, Esq., M.R.C.S., &c., Waterhouses, Ashborne.

JOHN HALL, Esq., J.P., Ball Haye Hall, Leek.

A. J. HAMBLETON, Esq., J.P., Butterton, Leek, (Chairman Leek Rural District Council).

ANDREW MORTON, Esq., J.P., Leek, (Chairman Leek Urban District Council.)

J. P. SHELDON, Esq., J.P., The Brund, Sheen, Staffs., (Chairman Leek Board of Guardians.)

SIR THOMAS WARDLE, J.P., Leek, and Swainsley, Butterton, Staffs.

Bankers.

The Manchester and Liverpool District Banking Company, Limited.

Solicitors.

MESSRS. CHALLINORS & SHAW, Solicitors, Leek.

Engineer.

JOSEPH FORSYTH, Esq., C.E., Fenton.

Secretary & Offices (pro-tem)

Mr. EDWARD CHALLINOR,
10, Derby Street, **Leek.**

PRINTED BY HILL BROTHERS, AT LEEK.

1904.

The Leek & Manifold Valley Light Railway Company.

Share Capital = £20,000.

FURTHER ISSUE

5000

£1 Ordinary Shares.

Hill Brothers, Printers, Haywood Street, Leek.

Above and below: Construction of Swainsley Tunnel. The locomotive is 0-4-2 Skylark, built in 1902 by Kerr Stuart & Co Ltd, of Stoke-on-Trent. It ended its days on the Snailbeach District Railway in Shropshire where it was scrapped in May 1950.

Below: Construction of the bridge over the road at the rear of the Crown Inn, Waterhouses. The lower photograph shows the line to this bridge. There was a delay in the construction of the line from Leek and it would appear from these photographs that the Waterhouses end was laid with narrow gauge track during construction work.

One of the two engines was named after Everard R Calthrop, **(left)**, the chief engineer, who was involved in light railway construction at the Welshpool and Llanfair Railway in Wales and also on the Barsi Light Railway in India, where a loco similar to the Manifold engines has been preserved. The other engine was named after John B Earle, the resident engineer **(below left)**. Also featured here is Godfrey Brewer, the mechanical engineer.

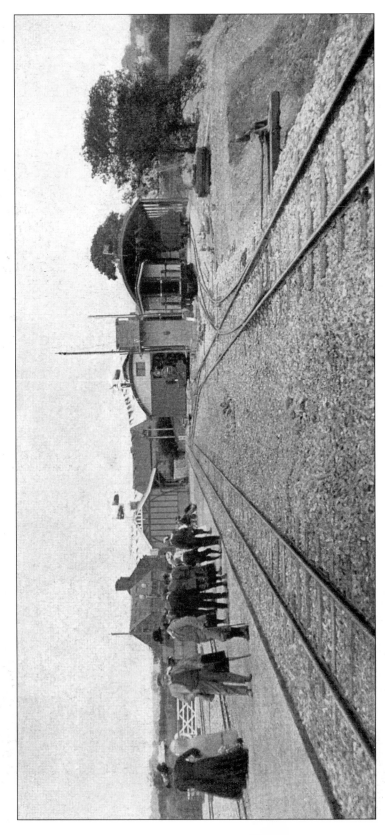

Open day, 27 June 1904 at Hulme End Station. The building with the flags was the station waiting room and ticket office. The middle building was the engine shed with the coach shed on the right. A water tower dominated the scene and other features were added after the opening including an old coach body for parcels and bikes, and a coal bunker. The coach shed appears to have been initially open sided. Note the platform was only 6in high.

Above: The coach shed, engine and one of the two low-sided bogie wagons (the other is behind it), used to transport guests on the open day. The seats are from the various stations, four to a wagon, with those from Beeston Tor and Grindon in view. Only two carriages had been delivered ahead of the opening.

Below: One of the ceremonial arches erected at Waterhouses on open day. It says *'Welcome to Earl Dartmouth'*, the Lord Lieutenant of Staffordshire, who performed the opening ceremony. Not seen was another poster which read *'Hurry up, NSR'* !

Above: Because of the delay in the connecting line to Leek, a temporary station was built near where the line crossed the Ashbourne-Leek road. Here is the telegraph office and the steam bus which brought passengers from Leek. **Below:** The open day train entering the Hamps Valley with both engines in steam.

Above: Ready for traffic. Grindon Station with a spur to a section of standard gauge line.
Below left: Approaching Thor's Cave and, **Below right** Visitors inspecting the new track.

THE STRAKER STEAM BUSES

The line from Leek was not opened until 1 July 1905, so for the first year of operations the NSR used two steam buses built by Straker & Co., of Bristol. They had iron-tyred wheels and the excessive vibration resulted in them being nicknamed *Earthquake 1 & 2*. They broke gas mantles in neighbouring properties and were restricted to Ashbourne Road, Heywood Street, Brook Street and Broad Street while in Leek. One of them was later converted to a removal van in Burslem, Stoke-on-Trent.

Above: Boarding at Leek Station. **Below:** Approaching the bus stop (see next photograph) at the bottom of Ashbourne Road, Leek.

Above: Loading up outside the Talbot Hotel, Leek. Passengers boarded at the rear. **Below:** There were three services a day and four on Thursday and Saturday. Here is *E223* at Lowe Hill Bridge near Leek. The bus used to frighten horses, necessitating the drivers to dismount and hold the bridle, as is happening here.

Above: The bus at Waterhouses outside the Crown Inn. **Below:** On the railway bridge in Church Street, Ashbourne.

Above: The first bus converted by Wedgwood. **Below:** Leek Station in a snow storm, taken at about the time the Waterhouses line opened.

One of the early trains at Bradnop Station after the Leek-Waterhouses line had been opened and the steam buses finally replaced.

North Staffordshire Railway.

LEEK & WATERHOUSES OMNIBUS SERVICE

COMMENCING JUNE 29th, and until AUGUST 31st.

The Motor Omnibus, in connection with the Trains on the Manifold Valley Light Railway, will run between Leek and Waterhouses in connection with Trains to and from the North Staffordshire System, as shewn below :--

TIME TABLE.

	a.m.	a.m.	Thursdays and Saturdays only P.M.	Thursdays and Saturdays Excepted P.M.	Thursdays and Saturdays Only. P.M.		a.m.	p.m.	p.m.	Thursdays and Saturdays only P.M.
Leek - - - dep.	8 50	11 15	2 15	5 0	7 25	Waterhouses - dep.	10 5	12 35	6 15	8 40
Bradnop - about	9 8	11 33	2 33	5 18	7 43	Winkhill - about	10 20	12 50	6 30	8 55
Bottom House ,,	9 26	11 51	2 51	5 36	8 1	Bottom House ,,	10 24	12 54	6 34	9 0
Winkhill - - ,,	9 30	11 55	2 55	5 40	8 5	Bradnop - - ,,	10 42	1 12	6 52	9 38
Waterhouses - arr.	9 50	12 15	3 15	6 0	8 25	Leek - - arr.	11 5	1 35	7 15	9 40

Passengers will be allowed to take luggage not exceeding 28 lbs. without charge at their own risk. Packages exceeding 28 lbs. will not be conveyed.

The Motor Omnibus will accommodate 22 Passengers only, and not more than that number can be accepted for conveyance ; and in all cases preference will be given to Passengers arriving and going forward by Train.

Stoke-on-Trent, June, 1904.

W. D. PHILLIPPS, General Manager.

Harry Lockett, Printer, Hanley.

The poster announcing the bus service, issued in June 1904.

NORTH STAFFORDSHIRE RAILWAY.

THE MANIFOLD VALLEY LIGHT RAILWAY

WILL BE OPENED FOR TRAFFIC

On Wednesday, June 29th, 1904

Train Service: Week Days only.

Miles		First and Third Class only					Fares Third Class	Miles		First and Third Class only					Fares Third Class.
from Leek		a.m.	a.m.	p.m.	p.m.	p.m.	from Leek	From Hulme End		a.m.	a.m.	p.m.	p.m.	●	from Hulme End
8	Leek (Railway Station) dep.	8 50	11 15	2 15	5 0	7 25			Hulme End (for						
	by Motor Omnibus			●	X	●		1	Hartington) dep.	9 5	11 35	2 30	5 10	7 40	Single Return
	Waterhouses · arr.	9 50	12 15	3 15	6 0	8 25	8d.	1	Ecton (for Warslow) -	9 10	11 40	2 35	5 16	7 45	1d. 2d.
Miles from Waterhouses							from Waterhouses	2	Butterton - · -	9 13	11 43	2 38	5 20	7 48	2d. 3d.
2	Waterhouses - dep.	10 5	12 30	3 30	6 15	8 40	Single Return	3	Wetton Mill - -	9 19	11 49	2 44	5 27	7 54	3d. 5d.
4	Sparrowlee - ·	10 13	12 38	3 38	6 23	8 48	2d. 3d.	4	Thor's Cave - -	9 24	11 54	2 49	5 32	7 59	4d. 7d.
4	Beeston Tor - -	10 23	12 48	3 48	6 34	8 58	4d. 7d.	5	Grindon - -	9 29	11 59	2 54	5 38	8 4	5d. 8d.
5	Grindon - -	10 26	12 51	3 51	6 37	9 1	4d. 7d.	5	Beeston Tor - -	9 32	12 2	2 57	5 41	8 7	5d. 8d.
6	Thor's Cave - -	10 31	12 56	3 56	6 43	9 6	5d. 8d.	7	Sparrowlee - -	9 42	12 12	3 7	5 52	8 17	7d. 1/-
7	Wetton Mill - -	10 36	1 1	4 1	6 48	9 11	6d. 10d.	9	Waterhouses - arr.	9 50	12 20	3 15	6 0	8 25	9d. 1/3
8	Butterton - -	10 42	1 7	4 7	6 55	9 17	7d. 1/-	from Waterhouses							from Waterhouses
9	Ecton (for Warslow)	10 45	1 10	4 10	6 59	9 20	8d. 1/1		Waterhouses dep.	10 5	12 35		6 15	8 40	
	Hulme End (for									by Motor Omnibus			Thursdays & Saturdays only.			
	Hartington)- arr.	10 50	1 15	4 15	7 5	9 25	9d. 1/3	8	Leek (Railway Station) arr.	11 5	1 35		7 15	9 40	8d.

● Thursdays and Saturdays only, Motor Omnibus and Train.   X Thursdays and Saturdays excepted, Motor Omnibus only.

N.B.--The Motor Omnibus will carry 22 Passengers, and only that number will be accepted for conveyance; and in all cases preference will be given to Passengers arriving or going forward by Railway.

MARKET TICKETS

will be issued to **LEEK** on WEDNESDAYS and SATURDAYS at Reduced Fares, viz.:

From Hulme End 1s. 6d., all other Stations 1s. 3d., Third Class.

LUGGAGE.--Holders of Market Tickets are permitted to carry Baskets or other Packages containing Eggs, Butter, Fruit, or other Market Produce, at their Own Risk, not exceeding 28 lbs. in weight, without charge. Packages exceeding 28 lbs. 1/- per cwt. with no less charge than 6d. But the Company hereby give notice that they are not and will not be responsible for any article so conveyed by Passengers. If required to be conveyed at the Company's Risk, Ordinary Rates will be charged.

On MONDAYS, THURSDAYS and SATURDAYS, Cheap Excursion Tickets will be issued at STOKE Station to Hulme End or any intermediate Station.

Fare 3/- for the Double Journey.

Important Notice to Cyclists.

Free Storage (at the owner's risk) will be provided for the day at Waterhouses, for the Cycles of parties arriving there by road and proceeding by rail to any Station on the Manifold Valley Railway.

Scale of Parcels Rates.

Parcels between Leek and Waterhouses or Hulme End, and intermediate points, will be charged as follows:—

Not exceeding - - - 10 lbs. - 6d. each.
Above 10 and not exceeding 20 ,, - 8d. ,,
,, 20 ,, ,, 28 ,, - 10d. ,,

Parcels weighing above 28 lbs. will not be accepted for conveyance on the Omnibus.

LUGGAGE.--Ordinary Passengers are allowed to carry 40 lbs. weight free all being personal luggage and not goods, merchandise, or other articles carried for sale, hire or profit.

W. D. PHILLIPPS, General Manager.

HARRY LOCKETT, PRINTER, HANLEY.

The poster for the line itself. It cost 1s 3d return between Waterhouses and Hulme End.

The Commercial Cars, Limited.

A NEW ATTRACTION FOR BUXTON !!!

MOTOR TOURS

For Residents and Visitors.

Road and Rail Pleasure Trips by Motor Char-a-banc and Train over the "Toy" Railway running through the beautiful

MANIFOLD VALLEY

Every MONDAY, WEDNESDAY & SATURDAY,

Until September 25th,

A service of well-appointed Char-a-Banes will run between Buxton and Hulme End. The Cars will run from the Market Place at the times shown below to Hulme End in connection with the Trains on the Toy Railway through the Beautiful and far-famed Manifold Valley.

Char-a-banc Fares Single Journey 2/-, Return 3/-.

In connection with these Tours, Cheap Return Tickets will be issued by the Railway Co. at Hulme End for the full length of the Manifold Valley Line (about 9 miles) to Waterhouses, also to Leek, and Stoke-on-Trent by the Trains and at the Fares shown.

	From		At S	At J			From	At		
			a.m.	noon	noon				a.m.	p.m.
Motor Char-a-banc	Buxton (Market Place)	dep.	9 20	12 0	12 0		Stoke-on-Trent	dep.	...	4 5
	Hulme End	arr.	10 20	1 0	1 0		Leek	arr.	...	4 45
Toy Railway	Hulme End	dep.	10 35	1 35	1 50			dep.	...	5 15
	Ecton (Warslow)		10 39	1 39	1 54		Sparrowlee	dep.	11 30	5 20
	Butterton		10 42	1 42	1 57		Beeston Tor		11 35	5 25
	Wetton Mill		10 49	1 49	2 4		Grindon		11 44	5 34
	Thor's Cave		10 53	1 53	2 8		Thor's Cave		11 47	5 37
	Grindon		10 58	1 58	2 13		Wetton Mill		11 52	5 42
	Beeston Tor		11 1	2 1	2 16		Butterton		11 56	5 46
	Sparrowlee		11 10	2 10	2 25		Ecton (Warslow)		12 3	5 53
	Waterhouses	arr.	11 15	2 15	2 30		Hulme End	arr.	12 10	6 0
North Stafford Railway	Waterhouses	dep.	11 35	2 30			Buxton (Market Place)	dep.	12 10	6 15
	Leek	arr.	12 5	3 0				arr.	2 15	7 15
	Stoke-on-Trent		1 E 8							

E—Saturdays only. J—Mondays & Wednesdays only.

Return fare from Hulme End to Waterhouses	...	...	1/3
" " " " Leek	...	...	1/8
" " " " Stoke-on-Trent	...	...	2/6

Children under 12 years of age, Half-price.

The Railway Tickets will be available for Passengers to slight from or join the Train at any of the halts on the Manifold Valley Line.

The Commercial Cars, Limited.

Cambridge Circus, London, W.C., September 1st, 1909.

HARRY LOCKETT, PRINTER, HANLEY.

North Staffordshire Railway and Commercial Cars Company, Limited.

PLEASURE TRIPS

TO

BUXTON

BY RAIL AND MOTOR CHAR-A-BANC,
Via the Manifold Valley "Toy" Railway.

EVERY MONDAY, WEDNESDAY & SATURDAY,

Until September 25th,

A Motor Char-a-banc service will be run by the Commercial Cars Co., Limited, (London), between Hulme End and Buxton at the times and in connection with the Trains shown below.

From		At		From		At S	At J	At	
		a.m.	a.m.			p.m.	p.m.	p.m.	p.m.
STOKE	dep.	8 10	9 50	BUXTON (MARKET PLACE)	dep.	12 0	12 0	5 0	
LEEK		8 50	10 55	HULME END	arr.	1 0	1 50	6 15	
HULME END	arr.	10 15	12 10		dep.	1 35	3 40	7 30	
	dep.	10 20	1 15	LEEK	arr.	3 0	4 18	8 13	
BUXTON (MARKET PLACE)	arr.	11 30	2 15	STOKE	arr.	4 18	...		

S—Saturdays only. J—Mondays and Wednesdays.

Motor Char-a-banc fares between Hulme End and Buxton Single Journey, 2/-, Return, 3/-.

In connection with the Char-a-banc service Day Excursion Tickets will be issued from Stoke to Hulme End at a fare of 2/6, and from Leek to Hulme End at a fare of 1/8. Children under 12 years of age, Half-price.

With a view to ensuring accommodation on the Motor Char-a-bancs Passengers are invited to advise the Chief Booking Clerks at Stoke and Leek Stations respectively by post-card the previous night of their intention to make the journey.

The issuing of Tickets in connection with these Pleasure Trips is subject to the conditions and regulations referred to in the Time Tables, Bills and Notices of the respective Companies on whose Railways, Coaches or Cars they are available, and the respective Companies will not be liable for any loss or damage, injury, delay or detention to the person or property of the holder caused or arising off and their respective Railways. The contract and liability of each Company are limited to its own Railway, Coaches or Cars.

HARRY LOCKETT, PRINTER HANLEY.

W. D. PHILLIPPS, General Manager.

Railway Offices, Stoke, September, 1909.

Posters for the charabanc service between Buxton Station and Hulme End, issued in 1909.

ROLLING STOCK

The ex-works photograph of ER Calthrop.

Facing page: The engines were 2-6-4 T's built by Kitson & Co., of Leeds. Initially they were painted chocolate brown and the coaches primrose yellow. This photograph was probably taken on the opening day. The man in the trilby is JB Earle standing in front of *ER Calthrop*.

A damaged photograph taken from *The Tramway and Railway World* of 1904 showing *JB.Earle*, the transporter car and carriage. The transporter allowed standard gauge rolling stock to be carried up the 2ft 6in gauge line. It was designed by ER Calthrop and first used on any narrow gauge system here on the Manifold Line.

ER Calthrop at Hulme End. *(Real Photos).*

Probably *ER Calthrop* outside the engine shed and adjacent to the booking office at Hulme End. The travelling crane on the right allowed some repair work to be done on site. Bigger jobs meant taking the engines initially to Stoke and later to Crewe. **Facing page:** *ER Calthrop* by the water tower at Hulme End. *(Real Photos)*

ER Calthrop having been returned from Crewe the 'wrong way round'.

A further view of *ER Calthrop* at Hulme End coupled to the transporter and two carriages in LMS crimson livery.

The two engines together after the switch. Despite fears to the contrary , *ER Calthrop,* served just as well.

JB Earle with a carriage at Hulme End.

Both engines adjacent to the coaling bunker. On the left is one of the 1st/3rd class composite coaches and one of the low-side wagons loaded with milk churns.

Above: *JB Earle* coaled up with about one ton of coal. The coal bunker on both engines was increased in height as clearly can be seen here.

Right: The company's wax seal for Waterhouses Station.

JB Earle (in front of ER Calthrop) taking on water. (Real Photos)

Above: *JB Earle* at the entrance to Hulme End Station. There were two height gauges, the other being off to the left of this photograph. **Below:** A double headed train with the open wagons converted for carrying passengers. This was usually on Bank Holidays, although the Gorsedd ceremonies held at Thor's Cave in September 1925 to at least 1928 attracted huge crowds of upwards of 2,000 from 1926 onwards. Extra trains were run to cope with the demand!

Above: Driver and mate on *JB Earle*. **Below:** The same loco pulling a coal wagon of standard gauge on the transporter at Hulme End.

Ex works photographs of the coaches. There were two sorts; a third class only coach, with the open platforms at each end, and a first and third class composite coach. The latter had the platform only at the first class end, with a guard's compartment at the other end. The coaches were 42ft long, 10ft high and 8ft wide. The width of the carriages was a bold move given the 2ft 6in gauge, but all worked well and the passengers were conveyed in more comfort. There were a total of four coaches, two of each type.

Left: The interior of the third class coach.

Below: The composite carried eight first class and twenty third class passengers, while the third class only coaches carried forty people. **Facing page:** A further view of the third class carriage looking through the open door to the platform.

A close-up of the composite coach in LMS red livery. The ornate logo L & MVLR was painted over and the vehicle given the LMS number 14989. Note the brake on the platform of the adjoining coach. (Photomatic)

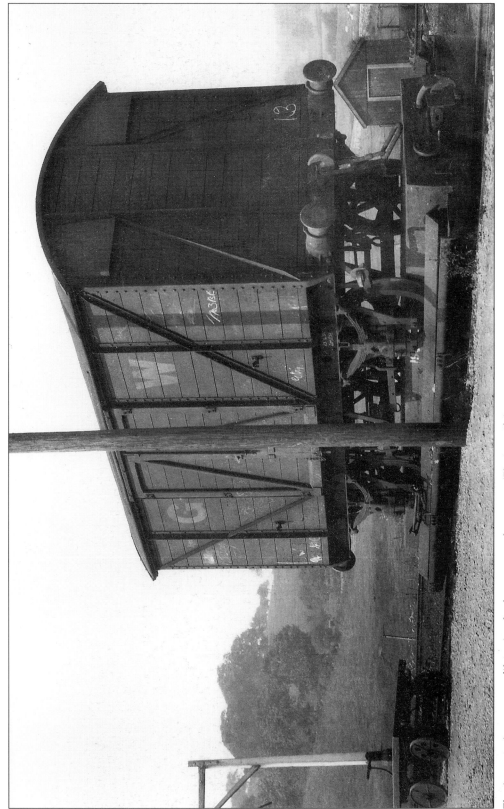

The transporter wagon with a standard gauge goods wagon. (Photomatic)

Facing page: Approaching Waterhouses Station in 1926 with a composite coach and one of the low-sided wagons loaded with milk churns. The carriage of churns appears to have been their principal use except when carrying passengers on Bank Holidays. (L & GRP)

Left and below: Views at Hulme End of the transporter car carrying a standard gauge wagon. These appeared in *The Tramway and Railway World*, July 1904. This simple idea enabled standard gauge stock to be carried and rolled off onto standard gauge metals at all stations except Beeston Tor and Redhurst Halt. The difference in height of the two rails was 10ins. To load the car, a lever was pulled which locked the car. The standard gauge vehicle was pushed on by hand and its wheels secured by screw wedges. The lever was returned and the car was then ready. It was intended that the car could also be used for carrying timber, milk churns, bulky items and interestingly, road vehicles.

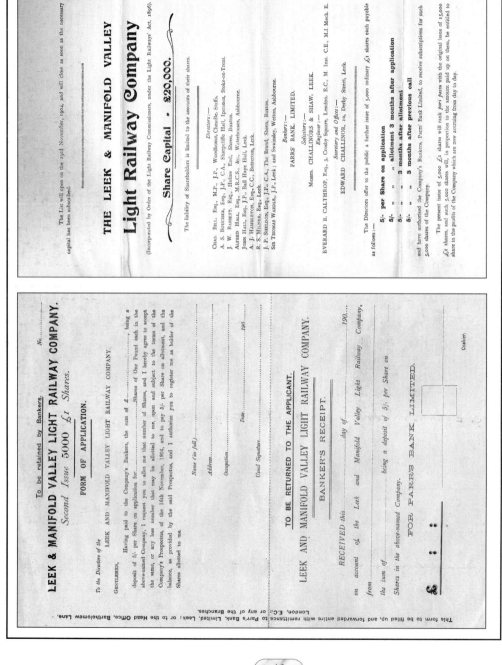

The construction of the line proved more expensive than had been initially thought and it proved necessary to make a second issue of shares. Here are the prospectus and application form. Additional to the £20,000 shares, the Company received a Treasury grant of £17,500, a Treasury loan of £7,500 and a County Council loan initially of £10,000 plus a further £5,000 received on 3 January 1907.

Examples of the AGM Report of the Directors and Statement of Accounts. The 1907 report indicates that at the end of 1906, the share issue had raised only £15,482. The number of passengers carried (in the year ending November) was:

	Single	Return
1905	10,347	19,149
1906	11,084	29,463
Increase	737	10,314

The diminutive narrow gauge train at Waterhouses alongside the Leek train. The little building is the booking office and the ladies waiting room. Notice the chimney above the guard's compartment on the first Manifold coach! The larger engine is ex NSR No 53, 0-6-4T, renumbered 2024 by the LMS and withdrawn in 1935.

Above: Waterhouses Station with the top of the steps which gave access to the platforms from the road. The signal box is in the background. **Below:** *JB Earle (?)* at Waterhouses.

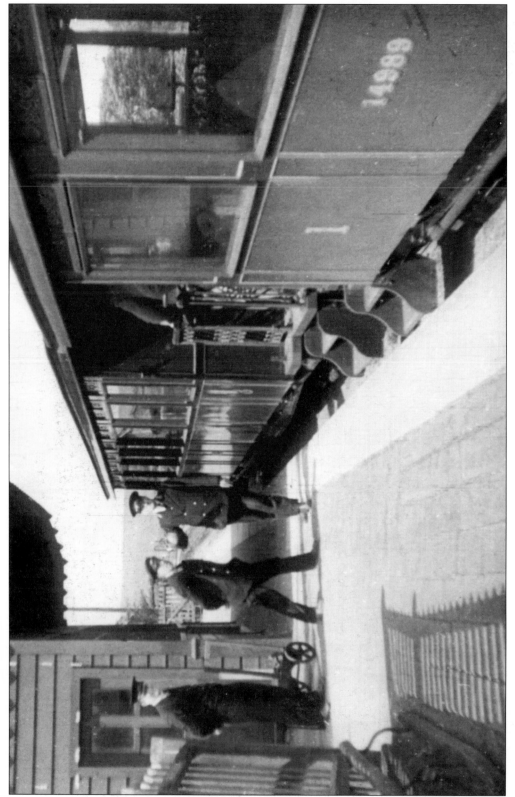

Ready for Hulme End, the coaches stand outside the Waterhouses cantilevered shelter. They are in LMS livery. The photograph was taken in 1933.

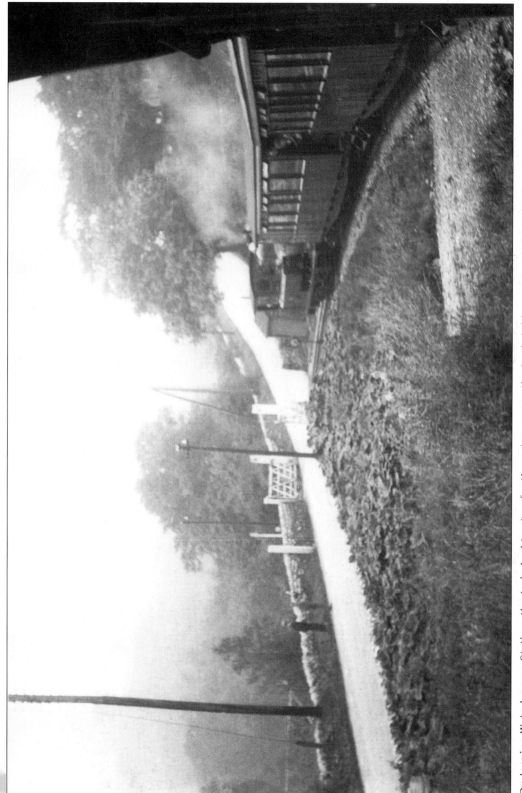

On leaving Waterhouses Station, the train had to stop for the gates across the Leek-Ashbourne road. (*L & GRP*)

Above: Heading for home. A group of people walking from the station at Waterhouses into the village.
Below: A wintry day at Waterhouses.

Two postcards of the line passing Brown End Farm at the entrance to the Hamps Valley.

BEESTON TOR.

IN THE HAMPS VALLEY.

ROUNDING A CURVE.

Below: Sparrowlee Station. Note the 6in high platform and (above) the standard gauge siding in the above photograph.

Facing page: Nithsdale, a commercial photographer of Leek, took several photographs of the train and surrounding villages and some of them are reproduced in this book. He produced a series of postcards consisting of three views, one of which was the Manifold train. (Basil Jeuda)

Beeston Tor Station. An old coach body served as a shelter and it is visible beyond the train.

Above: The beauty of the Manifold Valley above Weags Bridge and Grindon Station looking towards Beeston Tor with the line clearly visible. **Below:** Looking down towards Beeston Tor Station with the refreshment hut by the River Hamps.

Former Light Railway, Manifold Valley

Above: A lovely and rare photograph at Beeston Tor showing all the coaches in service with extra seating on the low-sided wagons and a coal wagon at the rear. (Derbyshire Life & Countryside. **Below:** An earlier refreshment hut at Beeston Tor. This is a postcard postmarked 1909.

Grindon Station with the standard gauge siding.

Above: Weags Bridge with Grindon Station beyond. During the summer, the river is usually dry between Wetton Mill and Ilam. **Below:** This photograph was taken from Weags Bridge and includes a wagon on the standard gauge siding.

A four coach set at Thor's Cave Station with the refreshment hut and waiting room.

Two further views of Thor's Cave Station. On the later and lower photograph, a new refreshment hut is in place and toilets have been added behind the waiting room.

Above: *JB Earle* pulls away from Thor's Cave Station. **Below:** Thor's Cave Station. L & GRP.

Above: Beneath Thor's Cave, the train leaves for Waterhouses. **Below**: Wetton village about one hundred years ago.

The classic view of the train approaching Thor's Cave Station.

Above: *ER Calthrop* leaving Redhurst crossing for Thor's Cave. The first wagon carries the initials RH & S: it is a coal wagon from the coalmines of Robert Heath & Sons of Norton and Kidsgrove. **Below:** A double headed train chiefly lost in its own smoke between Wetton Mill and Redhurst Halt.

Facing page top: Looking towards Redhurst Crossing. Redhurst Gorge from which the name was taken is off to the right of this photograph. **Facing page bottom:** Loading milk at Redhurst Crossing.

Above and below: Leaving Wetton Mill for Waterhouses the train passes Darfur Crags and the river swallets. **Facing page:** The view towards Wetton Mill Farm from the Hoo Brook footbridge, possibly taken some ninety years ago.

Wetton Mill Station,Manifold Valley,North Stafford Railway.

Above: An old NSR postcard of the train at Wetton Mill. **Below:** Wetton Mill Station.

Above: Wetton Mill Bridge, built in 1807 by the Duke of Devonshire at a cost of £184 after the previous bridge was destroyed by flooding. The railway siding is visible on the right. This section of the river was impounded as the millpond for Wetton Mill and the line of the weir may just be seen.

Above and left: Detail of the name plates and headlamp.

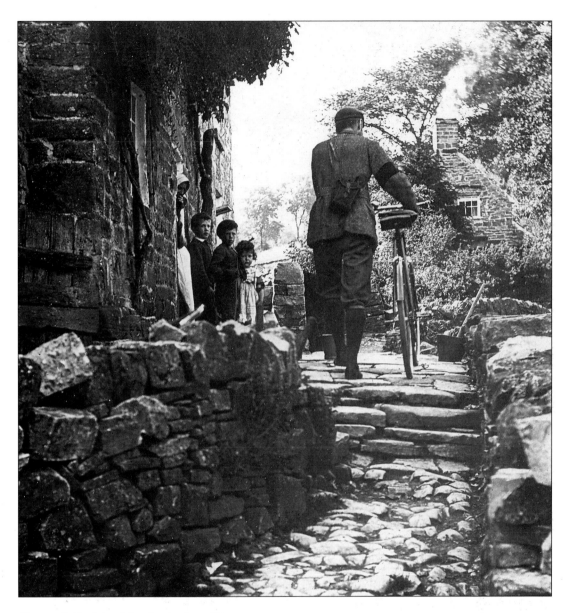

Above: Butterton at the beginning of the century. The cyclist is a Post Office telegram messenger. A telephone wire ran up the length of the railway line.

Facing page: Two views of Grindon village at the beginning of the century. The upper view is close to the church and the lower one shows the village pub. The railway was dependant upon the neighbouring villages but suffered because all had to be reached by climbing a hill. This was no joke if you were weighed down with shopping.

Above: South of Swainsley Tunnel. **Below:** The south portal of the tunnel. The tunnel is now lit.

Above: *JB Earle* approaching the tunnel at Swainsley. **Below:** The approach to Swainsley tunnel from Butterton Station. The bridge carrying the rails has since been removed.

ECTON, MANIFOLD VALLEY

Above: The line at Ecton Lea, showing Naylor's Temperance Hotel. The field in the foreground was used as a bowling green for a time. Above the two huts at the side of this field may be seen a collection of huts used by the navvies during the construction of the line. There was an outbreak of smallpox here in February 1903 affecting five navvies. **Below:** Butterton Station and Swainsley Hall. Note the standard gauge siding.

Above: Ecton Station with a temporary line in the foreground. **Below:** The train at Swainsley Tunnel.

Butterton Tunnel — Manifold Valley

Above: Former Ecton mine buildings before the opening of the cheese and milk factory. The entrance to Salts level may be seen plus the Boulton & Watt winding house on the skyline before the roof was lowered. The mine manager's house is on the left but the mine had closed in 1891. **Below:** A view after the cheese factory opened. **Facing page top:** This interesting photograph shows the remains of the Ecton Mine dressing floor on the right with the clockhouse smelter at the roadside and a cottage (now demolished) behind it on the bend in the road. **Facing page bottom:** Two low-sided wagons are carrying glass-lined milk tankers at the creamery.

Above: An old postcard of Ecton. The man stands between a little chapel built after the mine closed (and where Sir Thomas Wardle played the organ), and the mine's clockhouse smelter — it had a clock on the far side. The chapel had been the railway constructors site office. **Below:** Ecton Station with the passing loop and line to the stone loading dock to the right.

Above: A carriage and a standard gauge wagon on a transporter at Ecton. **Below:** A view of the Station from the former Dale lead mine. The clock may be seen on the middle of the three buildings. It was a reminder of the days when the copper mine worked a shift system.

Above: *ER Calthrop* at Hulme End. The bowler hatted gentleman on the left looks like Mr JB Earle. From an old NSR photograph. **Below:** The engine and coach in L.M.S livery at Hulme End.

Facing page top: *ER Calthrop* poses for a photograph at the creamery. The milk was bound for United Dairies, Finsbury Park in London. **Facing page bottom:** A milk lorry being unloaded at Ecton.

Above: Hulme End Station from the road in LMS days. The two adverts show the Trooping of the Colour in London. **Below:** Early days at Hulme End. Note the carriage shed is open sided.

Above: Coaling at Hulme End. The old coach body was used for storage of parcels and cycles.
Below: Although the glass was kept clean, the lamp was never used.

Perhaps the best view of Hulme End Station in later years. Standard gauge rolling stock stand to the left down from the booking office with the engine and coach sheds to the right. Note the travelling gantry, water tank and coal bunker.

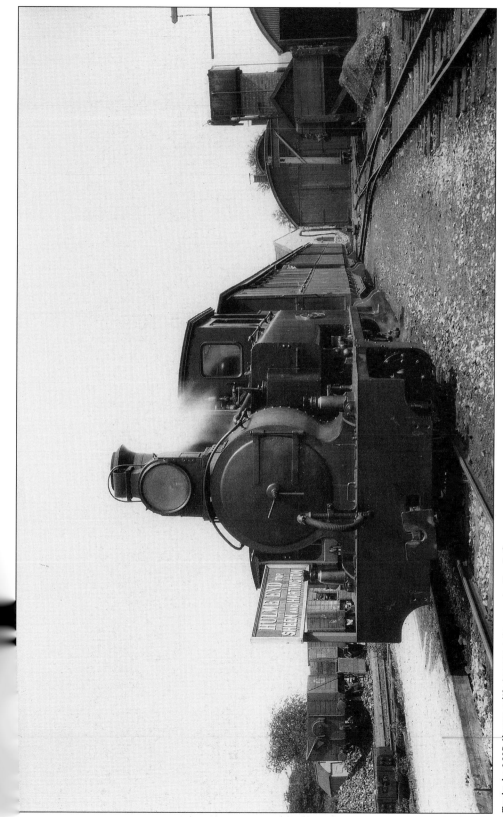

Train in LMS livery with transporter car to the left.

Light duties before departure. (Photomatic)

Hulme End booking office and storage shed.

Above: Hulme End village a hundred years ago. **Below:** A horse drawn sleigh between the station and the bridge at Hulme End.

Dr. to

The PORTABLE BUILDING Co. Ltd

Fylde Steam Joinery Works,

FLEETWOOD.

46A MARKET STREET.
MANCHESTER.

TELEGRAMS:-
"MOVABLE, FLEETWOOD".
"MOVABLE, MANCHESTER".
TELEPHONES:
20 FLEETWOOD.
1992 MANCHESTER.

BUILDING TRADES EXHIBITION
MAY 1895.
1898
DAIRY SHOW LONDON 1898 WORSLEY SHOW 1898
1899
WORSLEY SHOW 1899

Diploma of Honor
Brussels Exhibition 1900.
Honorable Mention Paris Exhibition. 1900

June 30th 1904

M The Leek & Manifold Valley Light Ry Co.,

10 Derby Street,

L E E K.

	£	s	d		£	s	d
To erection of One Passenger Station							
at Hulme End	137	11	0				
erection of 4 Passenger Shelters	160	0	0				
Do 2 Refreshment Booths	72	0	0				
Do 9 Station Name Boards @£3:15:6each	33	19	6				
					403	10	6
				£	403	10	6

By 13 June 1904 Paid on account 200 · ·
pd W Bussett 13.13 4 213 13 4

£ 189 17 2

Above: The invoice for the purchase of the Stations and refreshment booths.

ER Calthrop at Thor's Cave on track removal work in 1937. The last train ran amid snow and rain on 10 March 1934. The line formally closed on 12 March 1934.

DEMOLITION

Above: Demolition work at Hulme End. **Below:** The demolition crew pose for a photograph.

Above: *ER Calthrop* had definitely seen better days. In fact it had been stored at Waterhouses under canvas for about three years. **Below:** The train at Redhurst Crossing.

REDHURST CROSSING

At Waterhouses; the engine looks filthy.

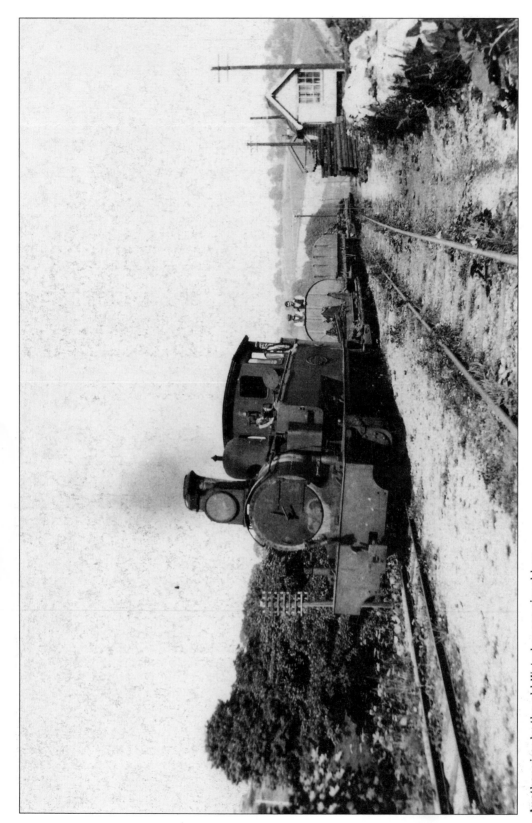

Another view by the old Waterhouses signal box.

Above: One final photocall for the crew at Waterhouses. The old coach behind the men features on the photograph below behind the transporter cars. **Below:** The rolling stock stored at Waterhouses.

Above and below: Two depressing views at Waterhouses after the removal of the light railway track. On the upper photograph, the old coach was the lamp and porter's rooms. The large building was the main station building and was used as the ladies waiting room, booking hall and office. The rear building was a shelter. The narrow gauge existed in the foreground. The lower photograph shows the view looking back from the shelter. (L & GRP). **Facing page:** The closure notice.